*O*ur purpose at Howard Publishing is to:
- *Increase faith* in the hearts of growing Christians
- *Inspire holiness* in the lives of believers
- *Instill hope* in the hearts of struggling people everywhere

Because He's coming again!

Thank You for Being You © 2002 by Howard Publishing Company
All rights reserved. Printed in the United States of America

Published by Howard Publishing Co., Inc.
3117 North 7th Street, West Monroe, Louisiana 71291-2227

02 03 04 05 06 07 08 09 10 11   10 9 8 7 6 5 4 3 2

Stories by Debbie Webb
Edited by Between the Lines
Interior design by LinDee Loveland and Stephanie Denney

ISBN: 1-58229-278-7

No part of this publication may be reproduced in any form without the prior written permission of the publisher except in the case of brief quotations within critical articles and reviews.

Scripture quotations are from the HOLY BIBLE, NEW INTERNATIONAL VERSION (NIV). Copyright © 1973, 1978, 1984 International Bible Society. Used by permission of Zondervan Bible Publishers. All rights reserved.

thank you for being you

thank you
for being you

a collection of poems, prayers, stories, quotes, and scriptures to say thank you

HOWARD
PUBLISHING CO.

thank
you

No one else could ever take your place in my life. Without you, this world would be poorer by far.

Dear *Charlie*,

Once in a great while, someone special comes along and makes a significant impact on my life. You are one of those special people.

There's something wonderfully unique about the way you express who you are—the way you laugh, the way you touch the lives of others, the joy in your eyes—that sets you apart.

You bless my life in ways you probably don't even realize, giving of yourself in countless thoughtful ways. I believe the greatest gift anyone can give is the gift of oneself, so I'm particularly appreciative of the ways you've shared yourself with me.

Thank you for being an outstanding person and for impacting my life. Thank you for all you are and for all you do. Thank you for just being you.

Sincerely,

Kevin

> Nobody else can do the work that God marked out for you.
>
> PAUL LAURENCE DUNBAR

We live in deeds...

We live in deeds, not years; in thoughts,
   not breaths;
In feelings, not in figures on a dial.
We should count time by heart-throbs.
   He most lives
Who thinks most, feels the noblest,
   acts the best.

—Philip James Bailey

Sandy's Release

Sandy's dearest friend was dying. Jeanette had been diagnosed with cancer five years earlier and was now nearing the end of an arduous battle. She was so tired—tired of the struggle to survive, tired of the pain, and tired of being weak and dependent on others. Yet, standing on the threshold of eternity, Jeanette lingered graciously, waiting for her friends and family to come to terms with her parting. Waiting especially for Sandy's release.

Those closest to Jeanette were tired too—tired of watching her suffer, tired of the losing battle, and tired from grief. But tired or not, Sandy just wasn't ready to give up her mentor and confidante. Theirs had been a long, devoted, and affectionate relationship reaching back over twenty years when Jeanette had taken the young and inexperienced wife and mother under her wing. Sandy had grown so accustomed to having Jeanette's wisdom and reaffirming love close at hand that now she hung on hard, refusing to let go.

Taking turns with Jeanette's husband, Sandy sat by her friend's bedside during the long nights of her final journey heavenward. Jeanette was wracked with relentless and intense pain, leaving her weak and requiring constant care. Though it was difficult to watch her friend suffer like this, Sandy couldn't bear being away from her. She felt a nagging pang of guilt about not giving Jeanette "permission" to leave behind her pain and slip into God's merciful embrace, but she couldn't bring herself to face the agonizing emptiness of life without her dearest friend.

The long, sleepless nights were underscored by the strains of everyday life. With a husband, four children, and a full-time job, Sandy had no time or energy for catching up on her work or her rest or for processing her grief. She felt she had no choice but to keep plodding, hoping to hold it together until this storm had stopped its raging.

But on Tuesday, at work and near the edge of exhaustion, Sandy felt herself falter. She had never been the type to cry in a public setting, but that day her eyes felt spontaneously and uncontrollably weepy, brimming with the tears she'd dammed up over the past weeks. Any incident, even the slightest provocation, would send them spilling down her cheeks in warm rivulets.

Sandy swiped at the salty streams in frustration. She was already having trouble concentrating, and the tears added frustration to distraction. She struggled to focus on her work, but her mind kept returning to the bed of sickness and the friend she loved. What if Jeanette worsened and died before Sandy could get to her?

Then Maxine, Sandy's boss, called her into her office. Sandy rose wearily from her desk. Pausing to gain her composure, she headed for Maxine's office, then paused in the doorway and stood quietly, waiting for instructions. Maxine looked up from the papers on her desk and, for a few seconds, just looked at her. Finally she spoke. "Come in, Sandy, and shut the door."

Entering and shutting the door respectfully behind her, Sandy felt a bit of trepidation. The only times doors were shut around the office were in performance reviews or disciplinary consultations. *What's going on?* she wondered.

Anxiety welled up in Sandy's chest as she stood on the opposite side of Maxine's desk with Maxine seated, looking thoughtfully at her. To Sandy, it felt as though her soul were exposed. Maxine's intense gaze searched her face for several seconds before she finally said, "Sit down, Sandy. I want you to rest awhile."

What? Sandy's thoughts were confused and tense. *Sit down and rest?!* Hers was a fast-paced job that required high-volume productivity, and management was always stressing the importance of efficiency. Working with a very lean staff, there was never a moment when Sandy wasn't extremely busy.

"Maxine," Sandy protested cautiously, "I'm fine. I'll just go back to work."

Maxine responded gently, but with authority: "Sandy, I said sit down."

Sandy sat. *How embarrassing,* she thought. She had worked diligently to acquire her reputation for hard work. Steady and dependable, Sandy had never let her emotions seep through her carefully polished, professional veneer. She had always been in control. But Jeanette's dying had pushed her over the edge of her endurance, and she hadn't been very successful at containing the sorrow that had rolled in giant waves over her heart.

Maxine refocused her attention on the documents in front of her as though Sandy were not in the room. Sandy sat quietly for a few minutes, then breathed a synthetic sigh of relief and said, "Maxine, can I go now?"

Maxine looked up and studied Sandy's face again. "No, you can't go. You haven't rested yet." Her gaze intensified and lingered even longer this time. "Sandy, you're too tired. I want you to sit here where I can be sure you're resting." At that, she went back to her work.

Convinced her boss must be displeased, Sandy inquired, "Maxine, is my performance slipping? I'm really sorry if that's the case."

"You know, Sandy, I don't really care about your performance right now," Maxine answered. "What I care about is your well-being. Now rest." The command was issued with the unique blend of sternness and compassion only Maxine could muster.

Relieved, Sandy sat quietly for a couple more minutes. Then, anxious to get back to the tasks at hand, she moved to the edge of her chair and said, "Thanks, Maxine. I feel much better. I'm going back to my desk now."

Maxine pushed her pile of work aside and leaned up on her elbows, giving emphasis to her words. "Sandy," she said, looking into the young woman's eyes, "you're weary in your body *and* in your spirit. Your dearest friend is dying, your heart is breaking, your reserves are depleted, and you're trying to keep everything running at its usual pace. I want you to sit right there in that chair until you have rested, until peace is restored. Don't tell me when you're ready to return to your work—I'll decide that. You are going to sit there until you rest." She leaned back in her chair with absolute resolve, folded her arms, and directed her gaze out the window.

The two women sat now in silence, and it was as though Maxine had stepped right into Sandy's grief and exhaustion and stood beside her. The gesture gripped Sandy's heart, and she felt the clamp in her throat as she tried to choke back tears. Somehow, Maxine's calm immovability was exactly the protective shelter and the release Sandy needed. Maxine emanated a strength of presence that seemed to reach the deep weariness in Sandy's soul and curl around it with an uncommon tenderness.

Sandy felt herself collapse into the back of the chair. A sob welled up from deep inside, and she began to weep. Maxine rose from her chair, came around her desk to where Sandy sat and, kneeling beside her, put her arm gently around Sandy's shoulders. "Go ahead, Sandy," she said in a low, soothing voice. "You need to cry. Cry until there are no tears left."

Sandy's final facade of strength crumbled, and she wept unrestrained while Maxine sat reverently, quietly watching over her.

After a time, the tears subsided and a peace came over Sandy's spirit that she had not known in a long time. Maxine gave her one last, tender hug and returned to her place behind the desk. "Now, Sandy, rest awhile," she said.

For forty-five minutes Sandy sat limply, with her eyes closed. Her resistance had been washed away with her tears, so she gave in to the provision Maxine was making for her.

She drifted through years of memories, reliving the relationship with her dying friend. She thought long about the legacy Jeanette was leaving and, though grieving the loss, she rejoiced in all they had shared. She reflected on things she had learned from Jeanette and loved her deeply for it all, and she considered how she could help her finish her race. And finally, she thought about Maxine and the precious gift of friendship she had extended in this time of sorrow.

Sandy rested more in those forty-five minutes than she had rested in weeks. Reflection brought peace. The sun was setting in her most precious friendship, and Sandy had been afraid of facing a new day without Jeanette in it. But now, even through the loss, Sandy's heart was filled with new hope and courage at the dawning of a new friendship. And for the first time, she knew she would have the strength to survive her broken heart.

Jeanette died on Thursday with Sandy at her side. Sandy had at last given her blessing to Jeanette's final flight. The release was a gift to both of them, and their parting words were simple and sweet.

As the daily routine of living returned, Sandy discovered that Maxine's insight and compassionate response during her sorrow were typical traits of her gracious heart. She got to know the warm, thoughtful person behind the business suit, and as she did, her pain and loss were eased by new memories and another devoted friendship that would last for years to come.

Sandy's Release

thank
you

Your unique way of modeling peace, contentment, hope, and faith makes today feel like a comfortable friend and the future a promised gift.

a blessing for you

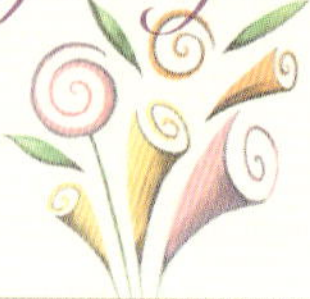

*M*ay God lavish you with laughter.

*M*ay the wings of your heart take flight.

*M*ay generosity grace your days

*A*nd consecrate your nights.

for being you

May your life be long and fruitful.

May lessons be gently learned.

May the hearts of those you've blessed

Send blessings in return.

A man leaves all kinds of footprints when he walks through life. Some you can see.... Others are invisible, like the prints he leaves across other people's lives.

MARGARET LEE RUNBECK

thank you

Your integrity and character are like snowcapped mountains in the heat of summer: refreshing, sturdy, beautiful, and magnificent even from afar.

The Lesson

My cot was down by a cypress grove,
And I sat by my window the whole night long,
And heard well up from the deep dark wood
A mocking-bird's passionate song.

And I thought of myself so sad and lone,
And my life's cold winter that knew no spring;
Of my mind so weary and sick and wild,
Of my heart too sad to sing.

But e'en as I listened the mock-bird's song,
A thought stole into my saddened heart,
And I said, "I can cheer some other soul
By a carol's simple art."

For oft from the darkness of hearts and lives
Come songs that brim with joy and light,
As out of the gloom of the cypress grove
The mocking-bird sings at night.

So I sang a lay for a brother's ear
In a strain to soothe his bleeding heart,
And he smiled at the sound of my voice and
   lyre,
Though mine was a feeble art.

But at his smile I smiled in turn,
And into my soul there came a ray:
In trying to soothe another's woes
Mine own had passed away.

—*Paul Laurence Dunbar*

It is our uniqueness that gives freshness and vitality to a relationship.

JAMES DOBSON

thank you for being you thank you for being you thank you for being you thank you for being you thank you for being you thank you for being you thank you for being you thank you for being you thank you for being you thank you

More Than Monday Friends

When Dave answered the phone, Carlee knew something was amiss. She was expecting Jenna to answer; Dave should have already left for work.

"Dave, it's Carlee. What are you doing there?" Carlee inquired.

"I live here," Dave responded with his usual humor.

"You know what I mean," Carlee insisted. "What's going on?"

"Jenna just left," he explained. "Mom called at seven o'clock this morning to announce that she had gone to the airport early and had gotten on standby for an earlier flight. You can imagine the panic that produced around here. She'll be at Columbus International by eight-thirty. Jenna has gone to pick her up."

"Oh no!" Carlee knew Jenna's mother-in-law had been scheduled to fly in at 5 P.M., and Jenna was counting on using those daytime hours to clean the house and start dinner. Dave's mom had a reputation for being a perfectionist, and Jenna had worried that she wouldn't measure up to the expectations Mrs. Reed had of her daughter-in-law. It was her first visit to the newly married couple's home, and Jenna wanted Dave to be proud and his mom to have a good first impression. "But Dave, don't you have to get to work? You haven't been there long enough yet to have vacation time, have you?"

"No, but I felt sorry for Jenna," Dave answered in a tone that revealed his affection for his new wife. "She worked late at the crisis-control center yesterday, thinking that she had all day today to catch up here at home. I'm going to take a day off without pay to help here. Jenna's taking Mom to the mall and out to lunch to stall while I clean house. They'll be home around two o'clock."

"Dave, let me help. You go on to work, and I'll swing by there and get the house in order. You can't afford to miss work. I know how tight things are right now." "Thanks, Carlee," Dave said appreciatively.

Monday Friends

Carlee's mind was already working. She was off for a personal day and had scheduled an appointment at a spa in Columbus. She treated herself to a day of pampering just twice a year. Her day out included a massage, pedicure, manicure, hair styling, and facial. But she couldn't imagine spoiling herself while her friend was in such a predicament.

Carlee and Jenna had met at the crisis-control center where Carlee was attending a grief management seminar just after her husband Glenn's death. Jenna was an intern working on her degree at the university. The two women felt an immediate camaraderie and soon became close friends. Carlee felt deeply grateful to Jenna. Her companionship, her positive way of seeing things, her faith, and her tender heart had done more to help Carlee recover from her loss than any counseling.

Jenna just had a way of giving of herself that was unique and refreshing. It was the little things that touched Carlee's heart, like the first time Jenna invited her to dinner on a Monday night. Jenna had said that she and Dave hated Mondays and felt like the week would start better if they spent time with a friend.

Carlee suspected that Jenna knew Glenn had died on a Monday night in a traffic accident. Now their routine get-togethers had turned Monday nights—once bitter and bleak—into the bright spot in Carlee's week. She wondered if Jenna would ever know how much grief those visits had spared her. Here was a chance to do some small favor in return.

Carlee canceled her spa appointment and phoned her housekeeping service, due to arrive in less than an hour, instructing them to meet her at a different location—the Reed residence. Then, reaching for her recipe file, Carlee quickly found the recipe for her famous beef stew. She tossed some spices from the kitchen cabinet into a bag and ran out the door.

The market on Second and Bailey had a bakery and a floral shop. Carlee bought a steaming loaf of sourdough bread, an apple pie that had just come from the oven, and a lavish bouquet of fresh flowers. Breathless with excitement, she sped over to Jenna's just in time to let in the housekeeping service with the key Dave had tucked under the mat.

Carlee began searing the meat as the vacuum kicked on and finished thickening the broth as the last mop was returned to the closet. She found Jenna's few pieces of china and set a beautiful table, complete with wine goblets and the sparkling cider she'd been saving for a special occasion cooling in a silver ice bucket.

She poured the stew ingredients into Jenna's Crockpot and plugged it in. The fresh bread was buttered and wrapped in foil, ready to go into the oven, and Carlee's work was finished by 12:55.

When Jenna pulled into her driveway at a quarter after one, she was nervous. She hadn't said anything to Dave's mom about his being home cleaning. He was supposed to be gone by two o'clock, and she would never know. But they had arrived forty-five minutes early, and Dave's car wasn't in the garage. *Where was he? He couldn't possibly have finished by now,* Jenna thought.

Trying to conceal her anxiety, Jenna unlocked the front door and flung it open, welcoming her mother-in-law with a flourish. She might as well get the disappointment over with so they could get on with their visit.

"Jenna!" Mrs. Reed exclaimed from inside the house. "I am *so* impressed!"

Impressed?! Jenna wasn't sure she had heard correctly. She stepped inside, and sure enough—the house was spotless, immaculate by any standards. The mouth-watering aroma of stew wafted from the kitchen to greet them, and a beautiful arrangement of freshly cut flowers brightened the room. Jenna couldn't believe it. Dave couldn't have done this. Dave *wouldn't* have done this. But she had a suspicion of who might have.

Mrs. Reed found a note lying on the counter, and as she read it aloud, it told Jenna all she needed to know.

Jenna,

You never cease to amaze me! I swung by with a dessert—you've told me such nice things about Dave's mom that I wanted to send a treat—but you were already gone, dinner was cooking, and you even had fresh flowers on the table! I'm impressed! But then, what's new? Relax and have a great time.

Love,
Carlee

P.S. Oh, and about the pie...consider it a Friday kind of thank-you for a Monday kind of friend.

Jenna's smile couldn't have been wider, and she was flooded with gratitude. She knew there had been no sauna or massage for her friend today. It was just like Carlee to swing into action, rescuing her friend instead of pampering herself. She felt certain she didn't deserve a friend like Carlee—but she was just as certain that she would never give her up!

thank
you

The good deeds you do are too many to number, but they all flow out of who you are. So thank you for being you!

Thank God for the way He made you. You are special, distinct and unique. You were not made from a common mold.

ERWIN W. LUTZER

thank you

Thank you for helping me see the beauty in everything.

To Kathleen

Still must the poet as of old,
In barren attic bleak and cold,
Starve, freeze, and fashion verses to
Such things as flowers and song and you;

Still as of old his being give
In Beauty's name, while she may live,
Beauty that may not die as long
As there are flowers and you and song.

—*Edna St. Vincent Millay*

Dear Heavenly Father,

I want to thank You for putting a very special person in my life—a person like no other I've known, and one who has touched my heart in a way no other has.

Where do I begin to tell You what she means to me? I could begin by thanking You for her depth of character, her purity of heart, her refreshing insight, and her unique perspective. Or I could start by saying how much I appreciate the reflection of Your goodness in her eyes, her genuine compassion, and her radiant smile. And there's so much more.

But You already know all this, because You made her the unique and beautiful person she is. So I'd simply like to say that I appreciate the way You've blessed my life by making her a part of it. Thank You for making her the wonderful individual she is. And Lord, please return a special blessing to her for so generously sharing herself with me. Help her to know how treasured she is, not for what she does, but just for who she is.

Amen.

I ALWAYS THANK GOD FOR YOU BECAUSE OF HIS GRACE GIVEN YOU IN CHRIST JESUS.

1 Corinthians 1:4

NIV